Woodburning Basics

Dick Armstrong

Schiffer Publishing Ltd

4880 Lower Valley Road   Atglen, Pennsylvania 19310

Published by Schiffer Publishing Ltd.
4880 Lower Valley Road
Atglen, PA 19310
Phone: (610) 593-1777; Fax: (610) 593-2002
E-mail: Info@schifferbooks.com

For the largest selection of fine reference books on this
and related subjects, please visit our web site at

www.schifferbooks.com
We are always looking for people to write books on
new and related subjects. If you have an idea for a book
please contact us at the above address.

This book may be purchased from the publisher.
Include $3.95 for shipping.
Please try your bookstore first.

You may write for a free catalog.

In Europe, Schiffer books are distributed by
Bushwood Books
6 Marksbury Ave.
Kew Gardens
Surrey TW9 4JF England
Phone: 44 (0) 20 8392-8585; Fax: 44 (0) 20 8392-9876
E-mail: info@bushwoodbooks.co.uk
Website: www.bushwoodbooks.co.uk
Free postage in the U.K., Europe; air mail at cost.

Designed by Mark David Bowyer
Type set in Tiffany Hv BT / Dutch809 Rm BT

ISBN: 978-0-7643-2675-2
Printed in China

Introduction

Like everything else, the world of pyrography has come into the age of technology. Fancy equipment is available that allows the woodburner to adjust the temperature of the tip for a whole range of effects, and offers hundreds of points to meet almost every burning requirement. There is nothing wrong with these tools and for some situations and some personalities they may be just the thing.

But for me I like the feel of the single tipped, wooden handle burner, whose only control is an on/off switch. It puts me in touch with the wood and the art in the same way a pencil does when I am drawing. And part of what I love about woodburning is the challenge of getting as much creativity as I can out of this simple tool.

This book grows out my years of experience in woodburning. It offers the basics that all woodburners should know, whether or not they later graduate to "high-tech." Because the equipment is reasonably priced it is within the price range of a young person just starting out, and the book gives them the first steps they need to accomplish before moving ahead.

After some instruction into the basics of the tool and its use, the book is organized with a basic, relatively easy project, a coastal light house. The pattern is created freehand, with each step spelled out. This is followed by an easy project, an old barn, and a more difficult project, a clipper ship, both of which include patterns. At the end of the book is a gallery of some of my work over the years. I hope it will inspire the reader to step out and try new projects on their own.

I hope that all burners, new and experienced alike, will take something away from this book, and that they will find as much joy in the art of pyrography as I have.

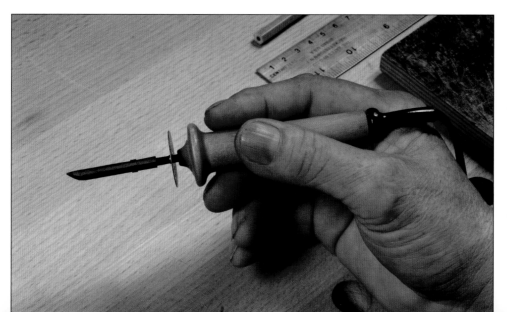

I use a single burning tool with a wedge tip. It is manufactured Hot Tool Inc. I like it because it is lightweight, small, nimble, and has a long life span. It is also reasonably priced. Higher tech tools are available, and some people love them, but for me this simple tool does everything I want.

I have constructed a stand using a piece of 1/2" inch plywood, about 4" x 12". Two pegs in the middle hold the tool, with the knobs keeping it from slipping out accidentally. The extra width of the stand provides stability as well as a place to test the heated tip. This particular board has seen 25 years of service.

The primary safety consideration is not to try to catch a falling tool! When you are leaving the work area, always let the tool cool in its stand for a couple of minutes before you go. The heated nib is very capable of burning you or causing a fire.

I like bass wood as a medium, but also use Oregon myrtle wood, cherry, or other tight grained woods. I prefer bass wood because it is light and offers a good contrast for the pictures.

I always draw the picture before burning it. It is easier to erase a pencil line than a burn line.

It is also easy to prepare. You can sand it on a machine or by hand. I use 150 grit sandpaper on a small sanding block. On harder woods, like myrtle, I usually need to use a machine.

A metal ruler is helpful for straight lines. This one has a cork backing so I turn it upside down to get a good contact with the wood. Just like with a pencil, I use it to draw the line with the burning tool.

With experience you will be able to draw a straight line freehand.

I use the forefinger of my non-tool hand to steady it as I burn.

I start a line with the tip. Not only is this more accurate, but if I make a mistake I only have a dot to correct.

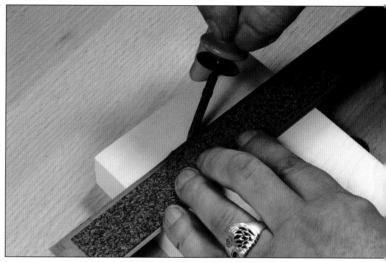

I want this line to be parallel with the edge of the wood, so I use the straight edge. It makes it easier to see and execute.

End a straight line with the heel down.

When using the straight edge, I usually stay on the point of the tip. It makes it easier to see where the line ends.

Erase the pencil lines. I use a kneaded eraser that allows me to shape it any way I want.

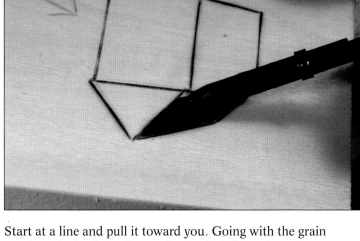

Start at a line and pull it toward you. Going with the grain creates a darker burn than going against the grain.

For artistic realism it is important to determine the source and direction of the light. I have marked it with this arrow.

I then turn the work and pull from the opposite direction.

For shading, the flat side of the tip should be dragged across the surface.

The roof portion is shaded.

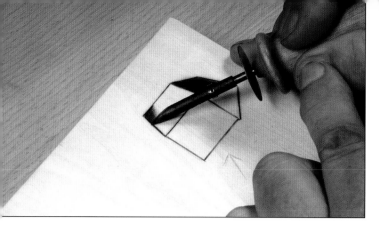

Follow the same steps on the wall.
Work from the line…

A wider, softer straight line is created by angling the tool a little higher and using the point and a bit of the edge.

going up the wall….

Pull the tool to create the line.

then turn the work and burn from the other edge. The difference in color between the roof and the wall is a factor of the hardness of the wood.

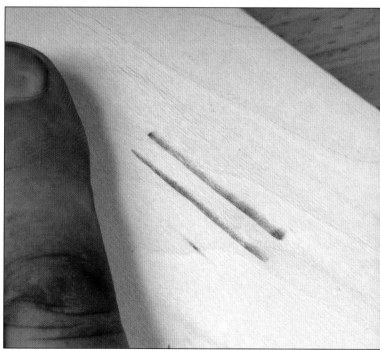

The result.

Using the same pen position you can create evergreen trees by starting at the top…

By going slower the trees get darker. The lightness of the tree makes it appear further away, while a darker tree appears closer.

and working your way down, moving the tip back and forth.

The result.

The result.

Deciduous trees are more complex and usually require a drawing.

Outline the trunk with the same laid-over pen position, going very lightly.

The foliage is created using the side of the tip and light pressure to create random short, crescent strokes. Nature is not perfect, so these should be freely applied.

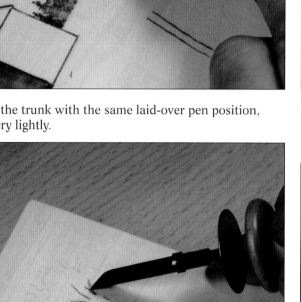

In the same way, add some limbs.

Progress

Add details with light touches of the point.

Remembering the direction of the light, shade one side of the trunk.

All leaves are not the same shade, so go back and darken some. Also darken areas of leaves to create shadow and depth.

The shadows transform the tree from a flat two-dimensional drawing to a realistic three-dimensional representation.

BASIC PROJECT:
THE COASTAL LIGHTHOUSE

For the basic project we will create a Pacific Ocean light house. The grain for woodburning always runs from left to right. Using a board that is approximately 6" x 6-1/4", mark the center of the board at the bottom…

The lighthouse will be centered on the center line. Visualize its position. At the bottom of the lighthouse make a mark 3/4" on each side of the center line.

and the top.

At the top mark 1/2" on both sides the center line.

Use the marks to create a center line.

Connecting these marks gives the traditional tapered shape of the lighthouse.

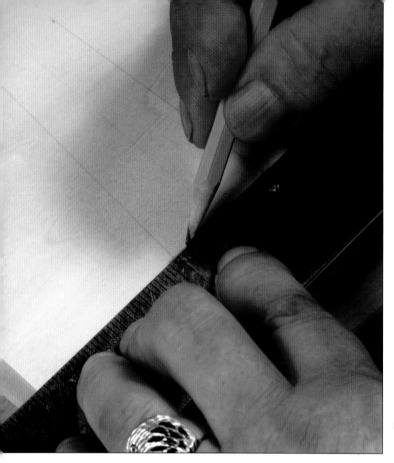

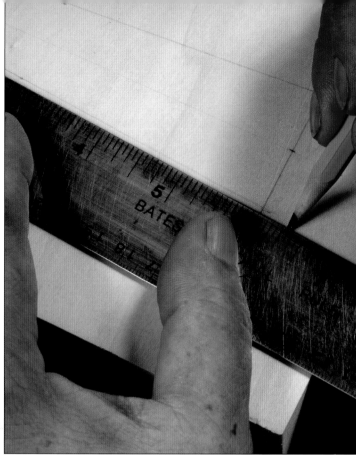

Draw the base line of the lighthouse.

Laying the straightedge parallel to the side of the tower and about 1/16" outside, draw a line to connect the base to the foundation line.

Parallel to that draw the line of the foundation.

Do the same on the other side for this result.

Measure 2" down from the edge of the board at the center line to establish the level of the platform.

Take another measurement slightly to one side…

And connect the marks, to draw the platform baseline.

From the center line, measure out 3/4" to each side to set the width of the platform.

Draw a line parallel to the platform baseline and approximately 1/16" above it to set the thickness of the platform.

Mark the width of the light at 3/8" to each side of the centerline.

Connect the lines to define the light.

Move up a little and mark the 3/8" measurements again,

Mark the height of the light at 1".

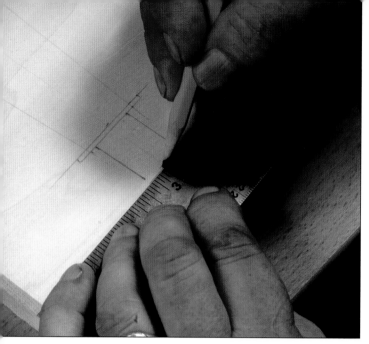

At the 1" mark draw the top of the light.

Measure up the center line 3/8" to mark the apex of the lighthouse roof.

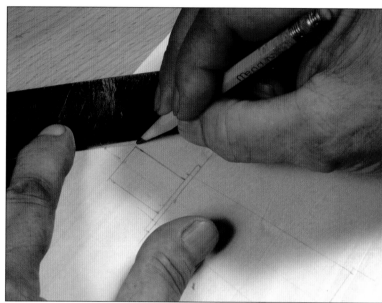

Draw from this line to the edge of the light, leaving a slight overhang.

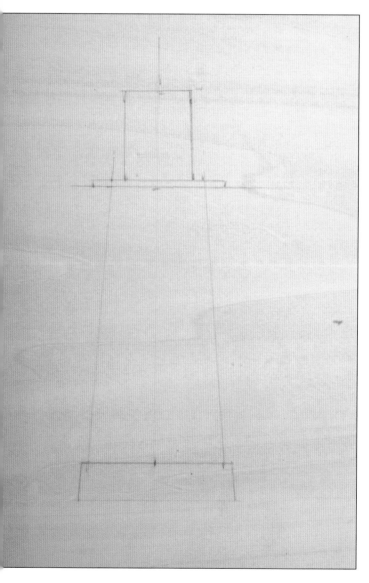

Progress.

Measure up 3/8" from the platform to set the line for the railing.

Draw the line of the railing.

Mark and draw a line 3/8" above the railing. This will be horizontal line for the panes of glass around the light.

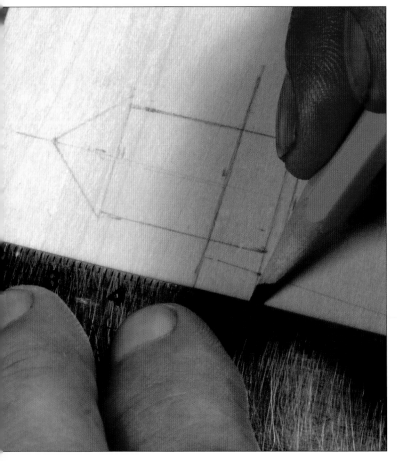

Draw in the balusters at each edge of the platform.

Vertical lines for the panes are drawn every 1/4", working from the side.

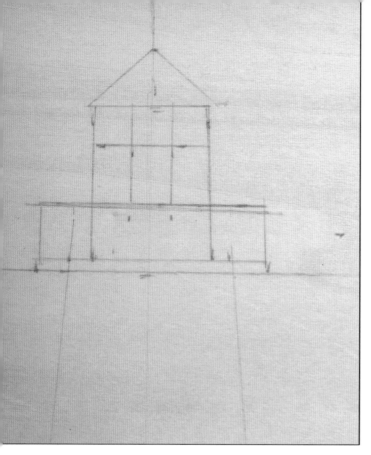

Progress.

Draw the remaining railing balusters. I am placing them about 3/16" apart, but you can do as you see fit.

Burn the outline. For the vertical lines I use only the point of the tip because I am starting and stopping at a horizontal line. It allows me to better see the starting and stopping points.

Burn the top line of the foundation, again using the point.

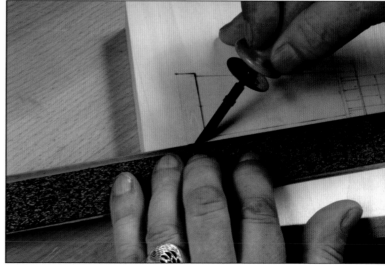

Burn the vertical lines of the foundation. The base will sit in grass, so we will leave the bottom line until later.

Burn the bottom line of the platform.

Burn the railing.

Burn the top line and connect the two.

Continue with the balusters. Here I am using the point of the tip.

Alternatively, you can use the edge of the tip to make the balusters. These are short lines and using the edge may help to make them straight.

Outline the light housing, using the point of the burner.

Continue with the roof, lightning rod, and window panes.

Draw and burn a window in the tower.

Short, freehand strokes create the grassy area at the base of the lighthouse.

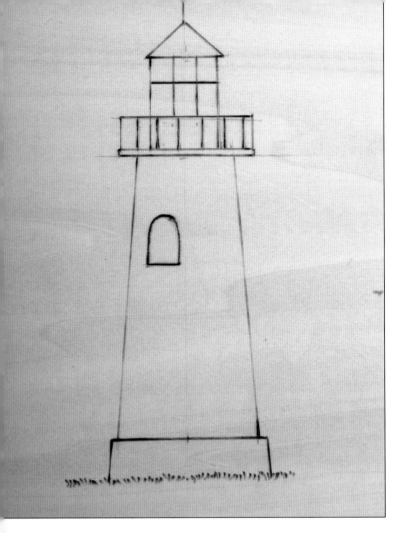

Progress

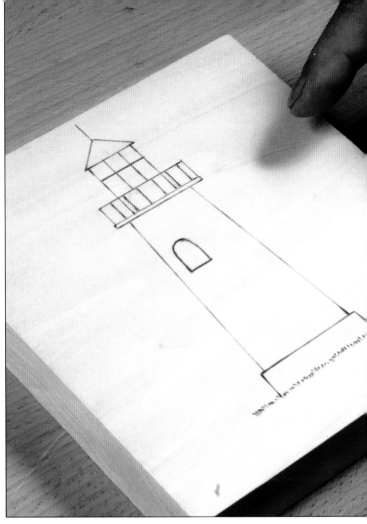

Determine the direction of the light. I want it from the top right as I look at the lighthouse.

Erase the pencil lines.

Since this is a round object, the shadow will lessen gradually as it moves toward the light source. Use the edge of the tip and, starting at the left line…

reduce pressure as you pull the tool toward you.

The result

This shadowing gives the impression of the tower being round.

Do the same from the other edge, but not as far since the sun is on that side.

Continue up the tower. The strokes may be repeated several times until you get the color you want. This is a much safer and effective way of creating shadows than trying to do the complete burn in one stroke.

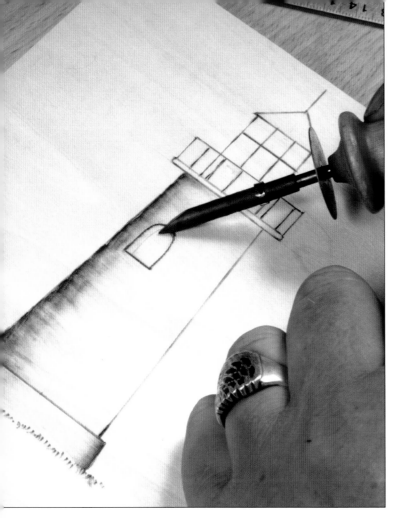

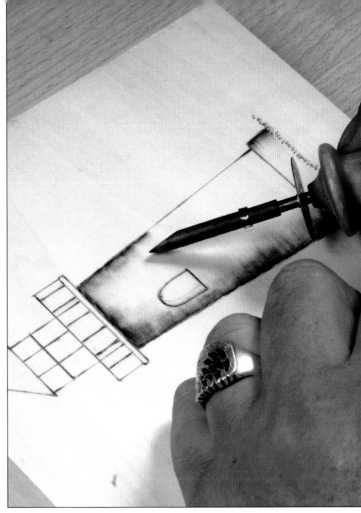

When shading, the tool sometimes needs to recover its heat before proceeding. I am now able to refine and widen the shadow.

Shade the other side of the tower.

The platform overhangs the tower, so shade from the platform down.

Blacken the window. Remember to leave the thickness of the wall unburned.

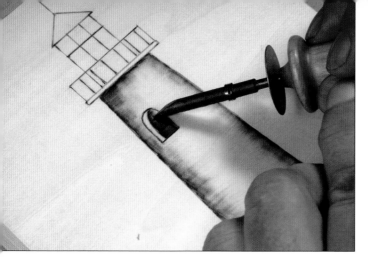

Now add a slight shadow to the top of the wall thickness in the window.

The result.

The result.

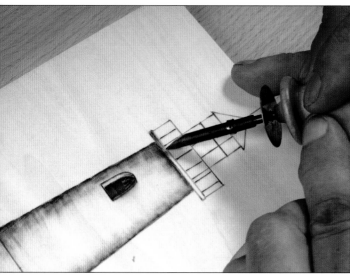

Shade the edge of the platform.

Next burn the steel base of the light. This is black so it will appear quite dark, though there will be variations showing its shape. The railings will still be evident because of their linear burning.

Each pane of the glass is shaded ever so slightly.

Add a slight shadow to the right (sun) side of the light and under the window rail.

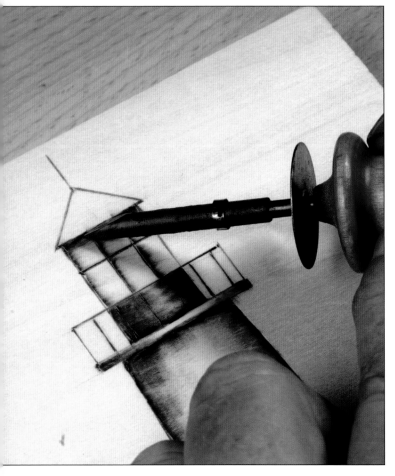

Shadow under the eaves of the roof.

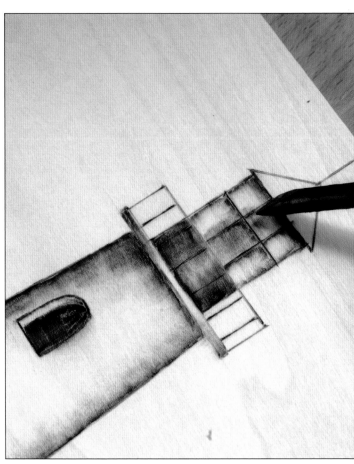

With the tool on its side make a slight shadow to indicate the light inside the glass.

Progress.

And finish from the other.

With the point of the tip add some seagulls to the sky around the lighthouse.

Shade the roof. Lighthouse roofs are usually black so this should be quite dark. Start from one edge.

With the flat side of the tool add some color to the foreground.

About 3/4" up from the bottom of the board I draw in a horizon line.

Lightly burn the horizon line.

A small sailboat will give depth to the image. Sketch it in with pencil.

Burn the sail boat. This is not a highly detailed drawing, the boat being some distance off shore.

The result.

Shadow in the ocean in a series of strips.

Lightly shadow the edges of the sails.

Finished.

THE OLD BARN

The second project uses a larger piece of wood. This is about 9" x 11".

Sand the surface with 150 grit paper.

I don't mind the lines in the grain of the wood. They help give character to the piece.

Transfer the image to the wood using graphite paper. It is available from art supply houses, and is nice because it is erasable. Place the graphite side down on the wood, place a copy of the pattern over it, and tape in place.

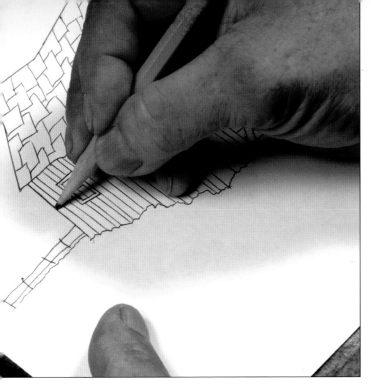

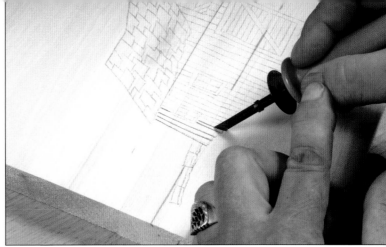

Go over the lines of the pattern with a pencil, using a fair amount of pressure. If you wish, you can use a ruler for the straight lines. After I do a couple of lines I usually lift the paper to make sure the image is transferring properly to the board. A hint: it may be helpful to use a colored pencil to go over the pattern. This will help you see what you have traced and what is left to be done.

The barn in this picture is rather dilapidated…no one is sure what is holding it up. For burning that means that it is not important to be precise in burning the lines. I start with the vertical lines of the wall boards.

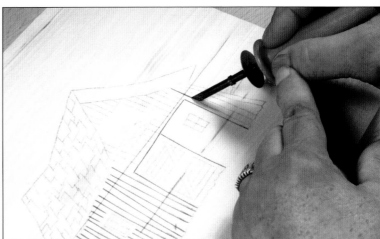

Continue with the openings and other lines. For the most part the tip edge is flat against the piece for these lines with a little more pressure on the heel as I get near the end of the line.

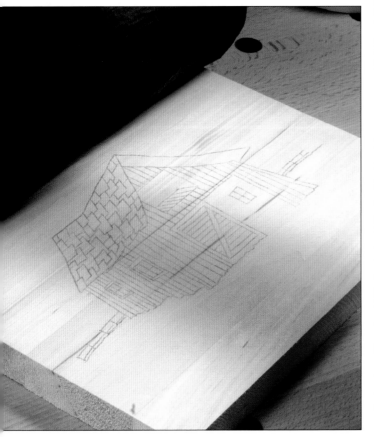

Before untaping the pattern, check to sure all the lines have been traced.

Continue in the same way around the details.

Nearly all the strokes are made by pulling the tool toward you…

The windows will be dark, so to make the stiles and rails stand out against them, I form them with two burns to give them thickness.

so turn the work as you go to make this happen.

The jagged line of the landscape is easier to follow moving horizontally than vertically.

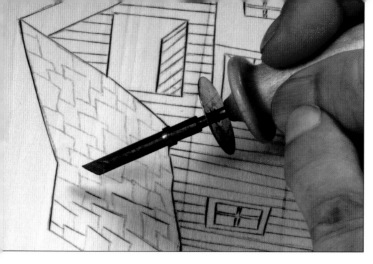

For the roof shingles I do all the vertical lines first…

then turn the piece and do the horizontal lines. I find this comfortable and efficient, but every one needs to develop his or her own procedure. For these short lines I my burner is angled right up on the tip.

Continue with the fence. The rails and posts of the fence will also be double lines.

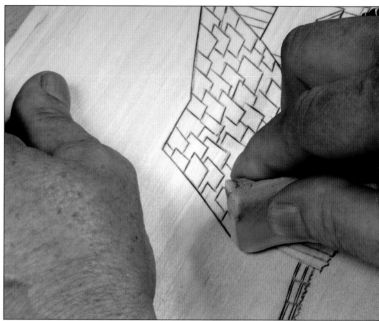

When the pattern is completely burned, erase the pencil lines.

Progress. You can start shading anywhere, but I like to start by darkening the interior spaces.

The small window panes are shaded using the side of the point.

It is helpful to establish the edge first before filling in.

For larger areas like the hayloft use the whole flat side of the tool. Apply good pressure and move slowly enough to create a dark shadow.

When shading a large area like this inside of the barn, you sometimes have to wait a minute or so for the tool to recover its heat.

Since this window looks outside, we do the opposite of the others, shading the rails and stiles and leaving the panes light.

Progress

The sun will be from the upper front.

Shade the underside of the eaves. Follow one edge of the pattern…

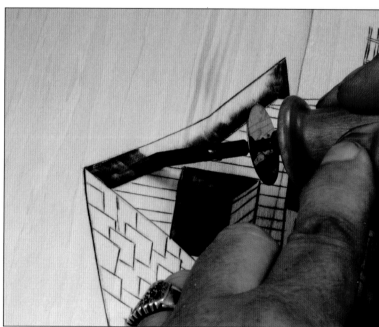

then turn the piece around and do the other. Use the whole flat side of the tip.

33

Fill in the rail fence.

The result.

A little of the fence line should show through the window.

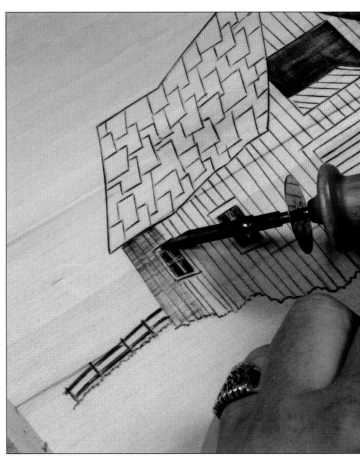

Add shadow to the shady side of the building. This should not be as dark as the interior spaces, so use a lighter touch.

You show a missing board by darkening the area further.

The result.

The result.

You can carry this technique to other parts of the barn, like here on the barn door.

Some wider spaces between the boards also add character. I do this using the heel of the tool and pushing away from me. This gives a nice dark burn.

Add some shading to the hayloft door.

Apply some light shading to the front to give it color.

Add shadow under the eaves.

Add hinges to the door.

Some shadowing around the door frame and the diagonal will give it depth.

As with the side, I widen some of the gaps between the boards on the front…

and remove some completely. This is done randomly and is a place to add some artistic creativity.

Add a shadow under the eaves. It needs to be parallel to the roof line and not too dark.

To detail the roof, start with some random holes.

Darkening the edge can also create a jagged, worn appearance.

Detail each shingle individually to give a more realistic effect.

Because this is a cedar shake roof, the shading starts by adding lines to the shingles.

When the lines are complete shade the whole surface of the roof.

With the basic pattern burned, you can now add some details. Perhaps some shrubbery at the corner...

followed by the foliage.

or a driveway.

With the basic foliage burned, add shadow.

Like the trees we did earlier, the shrubs start with the stems

Flowers are created by burning a stem and adding the blossom.

Outline the driveway using a squiggly line.

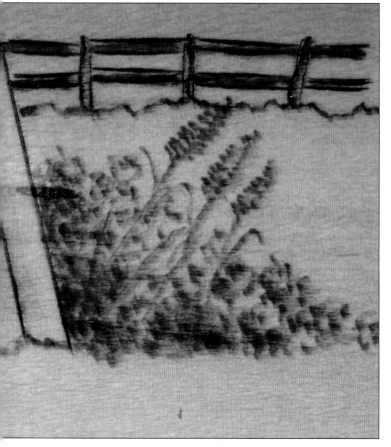

The result.

The farmer's truck left some ruts in the driveway. These are created with the flat side of the tool, the lines converging to give perspective.

Add some shading along the bottom of the door.

and the driveway is colored with a light touch of the flat surface of the tool.

Some tire track detail is added with the tip of the tool…

Some clumps of grass show the current disuse of the barn.

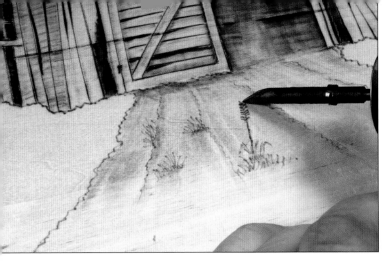

It is also not a bad place for a flowering weed.

With the shadow coming from the front right, the ground to the left of the barn will be in shade.

Some taps of the tip create pebbles and stones in the surface.

Blend the edge where the barn and ground meet, softening the line.

Progress.

Working from the edge of the driveway add some definition to it by color the surrounding ground.

Do the same on the other side, though lighter, since the sun is on this side.

When burning the board, don't use a lot of pressure.

Add some color along the fence line to the right of the barn.

One side should be burned more heavily to show the thickness of the board.

Some interest can be created by adding some of the fallen boards from the barn to the ground. Draw them in first.

Lightly drawn lines will add grain to the board.

43

Erase the pencil marks and…

the picture is complete.

The Clipper Ship

Transfer the pattern to the wood using graphite paper as before.

Continue around the hull of the ship.

I start with the bowsprit and dolphin spiker, establishing the lines using mostly the heel edge of the tool.

The result

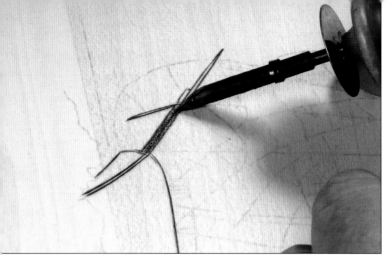

Darken the bowsprit.

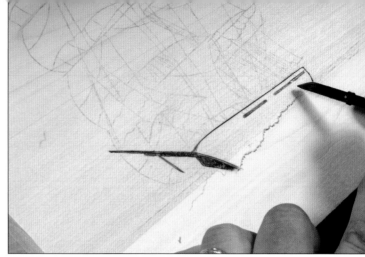

The water line is formed with a jagged line, not using too much pressure.

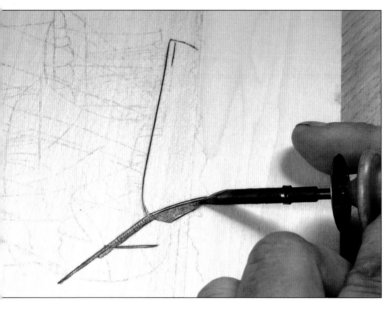

Shade the far side of the hull.

Draw the spritsail line, again making it a double line.

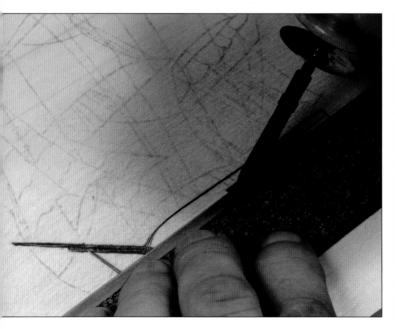

Burn the outboard channels. These are formed with a double line.

This has wood rings around it to which the sail is attached.

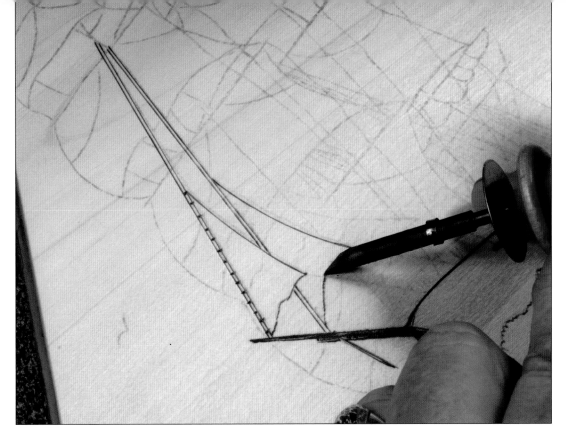

Outline the sail, the second spritsail line and sail...

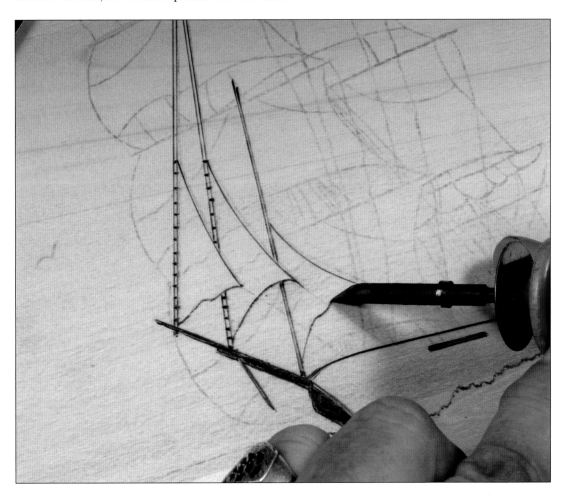

and the third.

Next I do the forward mast. I like to use a straight edge for this double line. It gets wider at the bottom. Be careful not to carry the line through a sail!

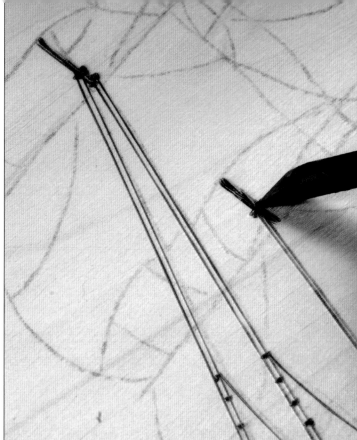

Add the anchor rings to the mast where the lines attach.

Fill in the mast.

Outline the topsail and its lines. Do not use too much pressure.

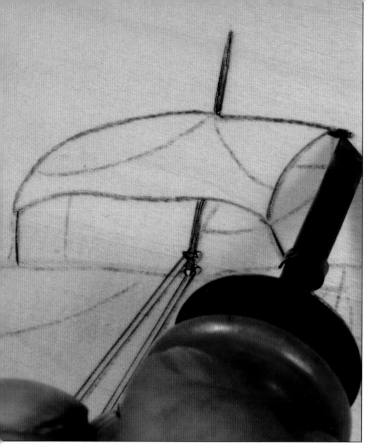

Add the end of the spar.

Do the same for the spar of the forward mainsail...

Burn the spar of the forward midsail. This is another double line, filled.

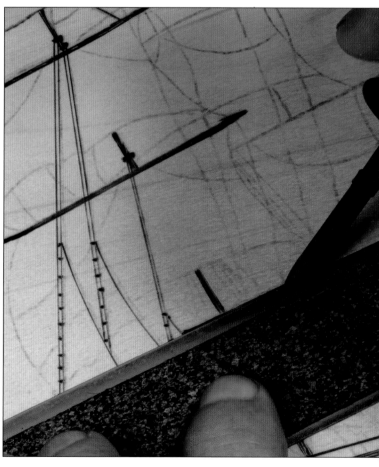

and the bottom sail. Again be careful not to take the line through a sail.

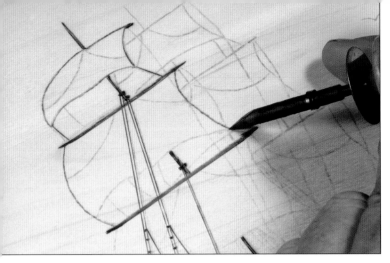

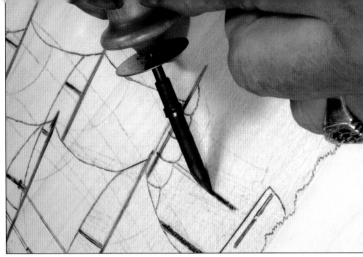

Outline the sails and their lines on the forward mast. These outlines should be made with a light touch. You don't want a heavy line.

and fill it in. While it can be rigged for sails, it often was not.

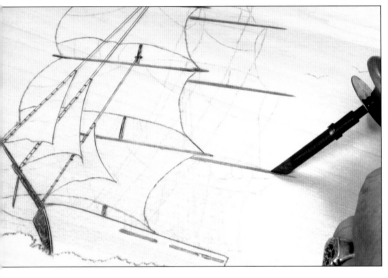

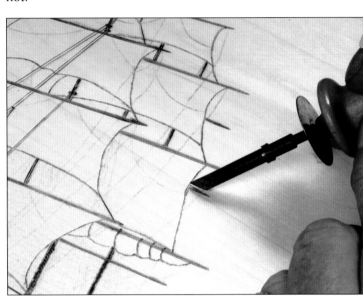

The same steps are followed on the main mast amidship.

Add the spars.

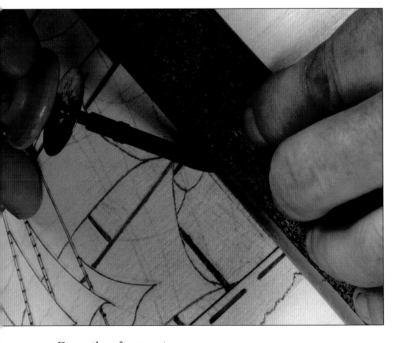

Draw the after mast…

Impressions of lifeboats are made by shading…

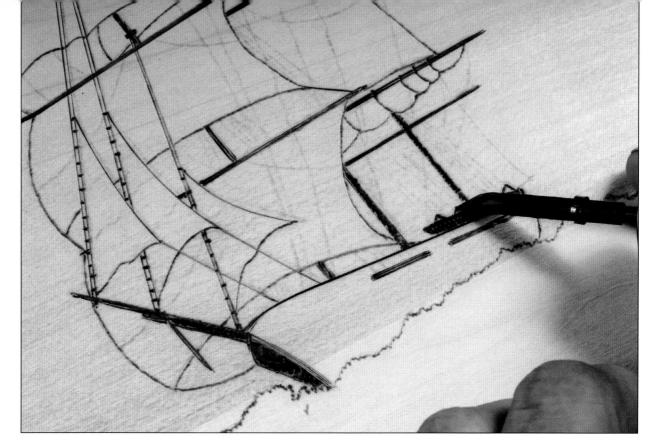

With the davits added above.

Add the mizensail boom…

the mizensail line and the lowered, crumpled mizensail.

The mast lines, however, are structural. They hold up the masts and are always taut. I burn them using a straight edge.

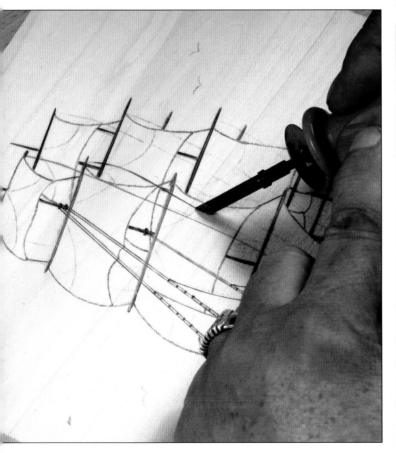

Draw in the lines from the sails and spars. These may be slack or taut, depending on the direction and strength of the wind. Here they are slack and I draw them freehand.

The cabin is formed with shadows, making a low box, and perhaps some things piled on top.

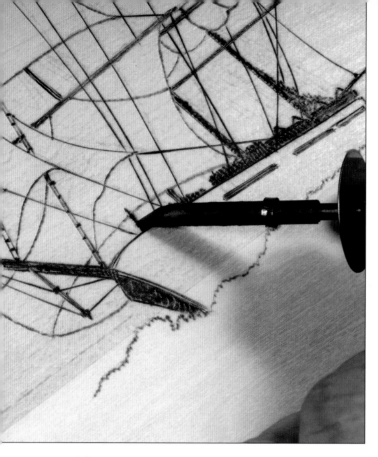

Forward from the cabin are other objects on the deck, again formed in shadow without much detail.

The forward sails have seams.

Finally a hint of a human figure or figures can be added.

These ratlines provide lateral support for the sail...

and cross members create a ladder for access to the mast.

Progress

Burn in a horizon line

Starting at the stern, begin shading the hull using long flat strokes

Add some seagulls.

Move to the fore and do the same.

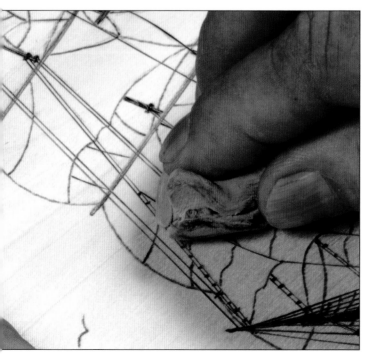

Erase the graphite marks.

A highlight at this point helps define the rounded shape of the hull.

Add anchor points for the ratlines below the channels.

The shading for the spritsails starts at the forward edge.

Shading of the sails begins at the bottom edge using the flat side of the tool.

The forward sail casts a shadow on the one behind.

The result.

The big sails are shaded from the bottom. They are made of panels of canvas, so I am coloring them to give the illusion of panels joined together.

The rear spritsail is close enough to cast a shadow on the bottom large sail, so a shadow needs to be added.

Moving to the spar, begin color down into the body of the sail as you did at the bottom. The area between the bottom and the spar will be lighter giving a billowing shape to the sail. Add shadow lines to indicate the panels.

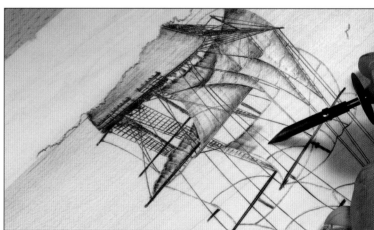

Do the other large sails in the same way.

Add shadow cast by the forward sails.

Use irregular short strokes to create the foam on the ocean.

Color the water.

As these accumulate they give the image of the wake created by the bow of the ship.

Look for missing elements, like the visible ratlines on the starboard side.

Finished.

Patterns

Gallery